STRENGTH SPEED AND ENDURANCE FOR ATHLETES

100 combative activities for partners

Written by **Jürgen Hartmann, PhD**

Edited by **Peter Klavora, PhD**
School of Physical and Health Education
University of Toronto

Sport Books Publisher Toronto

1112149

Canadian Cataloguing in Publication Data

Hartmann, Jürgen
  Strength, speed, and endurance for athletes

1st Canadian ed.
Translation of: 100 kleine Zweikampfübungen.
ISBN 0-920905-16-1

1. Hand-to-hand fighting – Training. 2. Physical
education and training. I. Klavora, Peter.
II. Title.

GV1111.H3713 1990 796.8 C89-094506-03

Distribution in Canada and worldwide by
Sport Books Publisher
278 Robert Street
Toronto, Ontario M5S 2K8

Printed in the United States

Contents

Introduction

The purpose of this book is to illustrate exercises that can be used not only in combat sports training, but also as part of any physical education or sports training program. The exercises chosen here do not have complicated rules and do not require special facilities, clothing or apparatus. They can be integrated into classes or training sessions at all levels and provide athletes a pleasurable and meaningful way to acquire competitive skills and to develop psycho-motor abilities and fitness. Moreover, their use can help instill in athletes a sense of conscious discipline, honesty, courage, the willingness to take risks and make decisions, steadfastness and responsibility and consideration towards opponents.

General Instructions

Although the combat exercises presented in this book are relatively easy to learn, they must be introduced with logic, consistency and method during training. Each athlete must be considered as an individual and work on exercises at an appropriate level.

Exercises which require relatively low levels of coordination and fitness (for example, exercises 3, 4, 6, 7 and 9) are especially suitable for beginners. Once the general foundations for higher performance levels have been laid by working on the less complicated exercises, one may proceed to more demanding variations. For example, exercise 100, which demands high levels of psycho-motor skill and fitness, may be prepared for gradually by mastering exercises 10, 11, 12, 26, 28, 29, 30, 51, 58, 59, 63, 66, 79, 85, 88, 89, 92 and 98.

The more complex exercises develop both physical and mental skills. When athletes are not bound to prescribed movements, they must formulate their own strategies and transform each situation to their best advantage, as they are required to do in competition. This is most encouraged by combining two exercises, each stressing a different skill or movement, into one. For example, it might be possible to combine exercise 46, which concentrates on attacking the opponent's leg, with exercise 66, in which the object is to lift the opponent off the floor.

Participants in combat exercises need to be mentally prepared and ready to use all their muscle groups. Every training session should begin with a warm-up consisting of stretching, calisthenics, games and partner exercises. The frequency, length and intensity of practices should be determined according to the objectives set and the participants' health and willingness to perform. Practice breaks and rest intervals are good times to stretch and perform relaxation exercises that accelerate recovery. Training sessions should end with a sequence of warm-down exercises.

Although these combat exercises are not governed by the strict rules of competition and are presented in an order that restricts the danger of injury, the following rules should be observed:

• Those competing should not wear rings, bracelets, chains, etc.

• All loose badges, studs or other dangerous items should be removed from sportswear.

• Many exercises require a soft practice area. Indoors, judo or wrestling mats should be used; outdoors, a sandy beach or soft lawn is sufficient.

• Nearby objects should be removed or padded to prevent injury; outdoor surfaces should be checked for glass fragments, stones, etc.

• Fighters may not grasp each other's fingers or toes, lock both arms around the opponent's head (unless one arm is also held), work against the natural movement of the opponent's joints or scissor the opponent's head or body with both legs.

• Only experienced and well-trained athletes should be allowed to throw their opponents to the ground.

• Some exercises (for example, exercises 64 and 65) should not be carried out if considerable differences exist in the weight and strength of the opponents. In general, however, differences in weight and strength allow for the better development of fighters' coordination, endurance and speed.

Table 1 presents the relative contribution of individual combat exercises to the development of different biomotor abilities, such as balance, speed, endurance, etc. The table should aid in selecting exercises for a training program based on individual or team needs.

Table 1   Relative contribution of combat exercises in developing psycho-motor fitness abilities.

Exercise Number	Reaction	Balance	Orientation/ Adaption	Strength	Speed	Endurance
1	++++	+	++	++	+++	+
2	++++	-	++	+	+++	-
3	++++	-	++	-	+++	-
4	++++	-	++	-	+++	-
5	++++	+	+++	++	+++	++
6	++++	-	++	+	+++	-
7	++++	-	++	+	+++	-
8	++++	-	++	+	+++	-
9	++++	-	++	+	+++	-
10	++++	+	+++	+	+++	++
11	++++	+	+++	+	+++	++
12	++++	+	+++	+	+++	++
13	++++	+++	++	++	+++	+
14	+	++++	+	+	+	-
15	+	++++	+	+	+	-
16	-	++++	+	+	-	-
17	-	++++	-	++	-	-
18	+++	++++	+++	++	++	++
19	+	++++	-	+	+	-
20	+	++++	+	++	+	+
21	+	++++	-	++	+	-
22	+	++++	+	++	+	-
23	++	++++	++	++	++	+
24	+	++++	+	++	+	-
25	+++	++++	+++	+++	+++	++
26	++	++++	++	++	++	+
27	+++	++++	++	++	++	++
28	++	++++	++	+++	++	++
29	+++	++++	++	+++	++	++
30	++	++++	++	+++	++	++
31	+++	+++	++++	+++	++	+++
32	+	++	++++	+++	++	++
33	++	+	++++	+++	++	++
34	+++	+++	++++	+++	++	++
35	+++	+	++++	+++	++	++
36	+++	+++	++++	+++	++	+++

Table 1 continued

Exercise Number	Reaction	Balance	Orientation/ Adaption	Strength	Speed	Endurance
37	+++	++	++++	++	++	++
38	+++	+++	++++	+++	+++	+++
39	+++	+++	++++	++	++	+++
40	++	++	++++	+++	++	++
41	++	+	++++	+	++	+
42	++	+	++++	++	++	++
43	+++	+	++++	++	++	++
44	+++	+	++++	+	+++	++
45	+++	++	++++	++	+++	++
46	+++	+	++++	++	+++	++
48	+++	+++	++++	+++	++	+++
49	+	-	-	++++	+	+
50	+	+++	+	++++	+	+
51	+	+++	+	++++	+	+
52	+	+++	+	++++	+	+
53	-	-	-	++++	-	+
54	+	-	+	++++	+	-
55	+	+++	+	++++	+	+
56	-	-	-	++++	-	+
57	-	-	-	++++	-	+
58	+	-	+	++++	++	++
59	+	-	+	++++	++	++
60	+	+	+	++++	++	++
61	+	++	+	++++	+	+
62	+	++	+	++++	+	++
63	-	+	-	++++	+	++
64	-	+	-	++++	+	+
65	+	++	+	++++	+	++
66	+	++	+	++++	++	++
67	-	+	-	++++	+	+
68	-	++	-	++++	+	+
69	+	++	+	++++	++	+
70	++	++	++	++++	++	+
71	++	++	+++	++++	++	++
72	-	-	-	++++	+	-
73	++	++	+++	++++	++	++
74	-	-	-	++++	+	+
75	+	+	+	++++	+	+

Table 1   continued

Exercise Number	Reaction	Balance	Orientation Adaption	Strength	Speed	Endurance
76	-	+	-	++++	-	+
77	-	+	-	++++	-	+
78	-	-	-	++++	-	+
79	+++	++	+	+++	++++	-
80	+++	+	+	++	++++	+
81	+++	+	+	++	++++	+
82	+++	++	+	+++	++++	-
83	++	++	+	++	++++	++
84	++++	+	++++	++	++++	++
85	+++	++	++++	++	++++	++
86	+++	++	+++	+	++++	+
87	+++	++	+++	++	+++	++++
88	+	++	++	+++	+	++++
89	+	++	++	+++	+	++++
90	+	++	++	+++	+	++++
91	+	++	++	+++	+	+++
92	+	++	++	+++	+	++++
93	++	++	+++	++	++	++++
94	++	++	++	+++	++	++++
95	++	+	++	+++	++	++++
96	++	+++	++	+++	++	++++
97	++	+	++	+++	++	++++
98	+++	+++	+++	+++	++	++++
99	+++	+++	+++	++	+++	++++
100	+++	+++	+++	+++	++	+++

Legend: Value of exercise

excellent	=	++++
very good	=	+++
adequate	=	++
poor	=	+
inappropriate	=	-

Developing Psycho-Motor Abilities

Athlete's psycho-motor abilities are important capacities that determine high levels of achievement in sports. They form the basis to guide and control motor activity and enable athletes to perform a motor task in a goal-oriented and expedient fashion. Various anatomical, physiological and psychological characteristics and abilities may be developed during different kinds of athletic training. In the following sections we shall deal only with those psycho-motor abilities which may be be developed particularly effectively by training using combat exercises. These abilities are reaction speed, balance, orientation and correction performance.

Reaction Speed

Reaction speed is determined by the accuracy and speed of motor responses to specific signals, whether optical, acoustic, kinaesthetic or tactile. With appropriate training, reaction time may be shortened, and the accuracy of motor responses may be improved.

Table 2 Example of a programme to develop reaction speed. Each practice session should last approximately 60 min. and include a 10 min. general warm-up.

Exercise	Duration of Exercise (in sec.)	Rest Between Exercises (in sec.)	Notes
2	90	10	
3	90	10	
4	90	10	Exercise is repeated with
6	90	10	athletes continually
7	90	10	switching roles.
9	90	10	
10	45	20	
11	45	20	
12	45	20	Continuous exercising.
5	45	20	
13	45	20	
1	90	20	Athletes switch roles after
8	90	20	45 seconds.
18	45	30	
25	45	30	Continuous exercising.
31	60	30	Athletes switch roles after
34	60	30	30 seconds. When an exercise
35	60	30	is completed in less time, it
36	60	30	should be repeated.
37	60	30	
38	60	30	
39	60	30	
43	60	30	Continuous exercising.

44	60	30	Exercise is repeated with athletes continually switching roles.
45	60	30	Athletes switch roles after 30
46	60	30	seconds (see also exercises
47	60	30	31-38).
48	45	30	
79	45	30	
80	45	30	Continuous exercising.
81	45	30	
82	45	30	
84	45	30	Exercise is repeated with
85	45	30	athletes continually switching
86	45	30	roles.
99	45	-	Continuous exercising.

Balance

Balance is the body's ability to maintain a state of equilibrium in spite of counteracting forces (static equilibrium) or to resume equilibrium following changes in position (dynamic equilibrium). Forces of disequilibrium may derive as much from a fighter's own offensive manoeuvres as from an opponent's attempts at attack and defense. The ability to maintain or restore balance is affected by such elements as the extent of counteracting forces, the size of the surface used for support and the position of the body's centre of gravity.

Table 3 Example of a programme to develop balance. Each practice session should last approximately 45 min. and include an 8 min. general warm-up. All exercises involve continuous exercising.

Exercise	Duration of Exercise (in sec.)	Rest Between Exercises (in sec.)	Notes	
14	30	10	Exercising on both legs.	
14	30	10	Exercising on right leg.	
14	30	10	Exercising on left leg.	
15	30	10	Exercising on both legs.	
15	30	10	Exercising on right leg.	
15	30	10	Exercising on left leg.	
16	30	10	Arms bent	On both legs.
16	30	10	and held out	On right leg.
16	30	10	front.	On left leg.
16	30	10	Arms	On both legs.
16	30	10	held	On right leg.
16	30	10	to the side.	On left leg.
16	30	10	Arms held	On both legs.
16	30	10	behind the	On right leg.
16	30	10	neck.	On left leg.
17	30	10	Arms bent and held out front.	
17	30	10	Arms held to the side.	
17	30	10	Arms held behind the neck.	
13	30	10	In walking position.	
13	30	10	In slow running position.	
13	20	15	From jumping position onto right leg.	
13	20	15	From jumping position onto left leg.	
18	30	20		
19	30	10		

20	30	10	
21	30	10	
22	30	10	
24	30	10	
25	30	20	
26	30	10	
27	30	20	
28	30	20	
29	40	20	Athletes switch roles after 30 seconds.
23	40	20	
31	60	30	
34	60	30	Athletes switch roles after 30 seconds.
36	60	30	
38	60	30	
55	60	30	
39	60	30	
48	60	30	
98	60	30	
99	60	-	

Orientation and Adaptation

Orientation requires the use of optical, acoustic, kinaesthetic or tactile stimuli to sense and analyze the position or movement of the entire body in space (e.g., in the fighting area) and in relation to a moving object (e.g., the opponent).

Adaptation is the ability to evaluate a situation, to select or develop a motor programme for changing this situation, to translate this motor programme efficiently into action and, where necessary, to make alterations to this program.

New situations may arise as a result of changes in internal conditions (e.g., insufficient strength or endurance), or of changes in external conditions (e.g., the actions of an opponent). When such changes have been anticipated, prepared motor programmes may be used; in the case of unexpected changes, combatants must be able to choose a relevant motor programme from their repertoire and develop it quickly into a meaningful response to actual conditions and demands. By using the following exercises, instructors can increase the ability of athletes to perceive and analyze situations accurately, to select or work out quickly an appropriate motor programme, to translate this motor programme into action and to correct it if need be.

Table 4   Example of a programme to develop orientation and adaption. Each practice session should last approximately 60 min. and include an 8 min. general warm-up.

Exercise	Duration of Exercise (in sec.)	Rest Between Exercises (in sec.)	Notes
10	45	20	
11	45	20	
12	45	20	
5	45	20	Continuous exercising.
18	45	20	
25	45	20	
31	60	30	
32	60	30	Athletes switch roles after 30
33	60	30	seconds. When an exercise is
34	60	30	completed in less time, it
35	60	30	should be repeated.
36	60	30	
37	60	30	
38	60	30	
40	60	30	
45	60	30	
46	60	30	
47	60	30	

41	240	30	Athletes switch roles after 120
42	240	30	seconds.
43	120	30	Exercise is repeated with
44	120	30	athletes cotinually switching roles.
39	60	30	
48	60	30	Continuous exercising.
84	60	30	
85	120	30	Athletes continually change
86	60	30	roles.
98	60	30	
99	60	30	Continuous exercising.
100	60		

Developing Physical Fitness

Physical fitness is required for sporting achievement and is determined by such physiological factors as strength, speed and endurance. These can be developed individually or collectively, depending on the selection of exercises and on the practice session procedures.

Strength

Muscular strength is the ability to counteract external forces or overcome resistance by means of muscle activity. Strength depends on the stimulation of muscles by the central nervous system, on muscle size, and on biochemical processes, including fatigue, taking place in the working muscle.

It is possible to distinguish between maximum strength, power and muscular endurance, which are closely related not only to each other, but also to speed and endurance.

Maximum strength Maximum strength refers to the largest force a muscle or a group of muscles can develop in one contraction. This is demonstrated, for example, in the largest load an athlete can lift in one attempt. Maximum strength is necessary where exceptional external resistance has to be overcome, for example, in weightlifting, wrestling, football blocking, etc. Its importance in athletic performance becomes smaller as the resistance that must be tackled is reduced and where competitions last longer. During maximum-strength training, athletes work against resistance requiring 70 to 100 per cent of their maximum strength. Each exercise series is made up of 2 to 5 repetitions and rest intervals between series are relatively long to allow full recovery.

Power Power is the ability to overcome resistance by a high speed of contraction. It is a product of two abilities—motor speed and strength: Power is important to achieve high velocity push-offs, throws or take-offs in games, quick actions in individual and team contests, acceleration in races, etc. During power training, athletes work quickly or explosively against moderate resistance requiring 35 to 70 per cent of their maximum strength. Each exercise should be repeated 6 to 10 times with resistance at this level. The rest interval between each series must be long enough to allow for sufficient recovery.

Muscular Endurance Muscular endurance is the ability to resist fatigue in performances requiring relatively high degrees of strength over a long period of time. Like power, it also requires strength. Endurance is particularly important to performance in events where exceptional resistance must be overcome over longer time periods, e.g., in rowing, cross-country skiing or swimming. During endurance training, athletes must cope with low levels of resistance, requiring 25 to 40 per cent of their maximum strength, within a wide activity range. Rest intervals between the lengthy exercises or series are relatively short.

Thirty combat exercises (exercises 49-78) are designed for strength training. These exercises primarily promote maximum strength development. However, the exercises designed for speed development and endurance training (Exercises 79-100) also have a considerable influence on the improvement of power and endurance.

Table 5   Examples of a programme to develop maximum strength. The duration of a practice session is approximately 60 min., including a 10 min. warm-up.

Exercise	Duration of Exercise (in sec.)	Rest Between Exercises (in sec.)	Notes	
49	40	30		
51	40	30		
52	40	30	Continuous exercising.	
53	40	30		
55	40	30		
50	40	30		
54	40	20		Both hands.
54	40	20		Right hand.
54	40	20	After 20	Left hands.
56	40	20	seconds,	Right fists.
56	40	20	athletes	Left fists.
57	40	20	switch	Right hands.
57	40	20	roles.	Left hands.
58	60	60		
59	60	60	After 30 seconds, athletes	
60	60	60	switch roles; a maximum of	
61	60	60	5 repetitions to be carried	
62	60	60	out during this time.	
63	60	60		
66	60	60		
64	40	60		
67	40	60	Continuous exercising.	
68	40	40		
69	40	30	Athletes switch roles after	
70	40	30	20 seconds.	

65	60	90	See notes on exercises 58 to 66.	Hands around waist.
65	60	90		
71	60	90		Hands around legs.

72	40	20		
77	40	20	Athletes switch roles after 20 seconds.	
78	40	20		

73	40	30		Right leg.
74	40	20	Continuous exercising.	Left leg.
74	40	20		Right leg.
75	40	20		Left leg.
75	40			Right leg.

Speed

Speed is the ability to fulfil a motor task in the shortest amount of time.

The quality of speed depends on the agility of the nervous processes, power, the stretch, elasticity and recovery levels of muscles, movement skills, and will power. Speed is one of the deciding factors for performance in many sports, and especially in the starting and accelerating phases of rowing, canoeing, skating, etc.

During speed training, high to maximum motor speed levels are required over a short period of time. Rest intervals between the exercises or series are relatively long, to allow complete recovery.

Table 6 Example of a programme to develop motor speed. The duration of a practice session is 30 minutes, including a relatively fatigue-free 5 minute warm-up.

Exercise	Duration of Exercise (in sec.)	Rest Between Exercises (in sec.)	Notes	
1	40	20		
2	40	20		
3	40	20	Athletes	
6	40	20	change	Catching with :
4	40	15	roles	both hands.
4	40	15	after	right hand.
4	40	15	20 seconds.	left hand.
7	40	15		
9	40	15		
8	40	20		
10	25	25		
11	25	25		
12	25	25		
5	20	25		
25	20	25		
13	20	20	Continuous exercising.	From walking position.
79	20	25		
80	20	25		From sitting position.
80	20	25		From bench position.
81	30	40		From attention.
81	30	40		From sitting position.
82	20	30		
83	20	30		
84	20	30		
85	30	30		From standing position.

23

	Duration of Exercise (in sec.)	Rest Between Exercises (in sec.)	Notes
85	30	30	After 15 seconds, athletes switch roles.	From deep kneebend position.
85	30	30		From push-up position.
86	30	-		

Endurance

Endurance is the capacity to resist fatigue. It is especially important during lengthy sporting activity, both in competition and training. Endurance is also essential to ensure quick recovery following a hard workout.

All types of movement carried out at moderate to high levels over longer periods of time develop endurance. Endurance relates to the functional efficiency of the cardio-vascular, metabolic, nervous and hormonal systems and to muscular coordination. Furthermore, endurance depends very much on an athlete's mental abilities, particularly on will power.

Table 7 Example of a very intensive programme to develop endurance. Duration of exercising is approximately 90 min., including an intensive 10 min. warm-up. Each exercise is repeated until the time allotted is over.

Exercise	Duration of Exercise (in sec.)	Rest Between Exercises (in sec.)	Notes
31	180	90	
36	180	90	Athletes switch roles after
38	180	90	90 seconds.
93	180	90	

39	120	60	Continuous	
48	120	60	exercising.	
87	45	45		Running, jumping to the right.
87	45	45		

87	45	45		Jumping to the right.
87	45	45		Running in push-up position.
88	120	60		With right arm.
88	120	60		With left arm.
88	120	60		With both arms.
89	120	60		With right arm.
89	120	60		With left arm.
90	120	60		
91	120	60		
92	120	60	Continuous	
94	120	60	exercising.	
95	120	60		
96	120	60		
97	120	60		
98	120	60		With right leg.
98	120	60		With left leg.
99	120	60		With right leg.
99	120	60		With left leg.
100	120	-		

Simultaneous Development of Psycho-Motor Abilities and Fitness

Whereas the exercise programmes above are useful to develop particular psycho-motor abilities, the following programmes are designed to develop all these abilities together. These programmes can be widely applied, whether in school and community centre activities or in competitive sports training. The programme suggested in Table 9, for example, can be carried out in a very limited area and requires no particular sporting clothing. It can be used, for example, to loosen up after hours in the car, in the office, or lengthy activity. Exercises to develop reaction speed and strength (up to exercise 78) may be carried out in sitting position.

Table 8   Example of a program to develop both psycho-motor abilities and fitness. The duration of a practice session is approximately 60 min., including a general 6 min. warm-up.

Exercise	Duration of Exercise (in sec.)	Rest Between Exercises (in sec.)	Notes
3	40	10	
6	40	10	
4	40	10	After 20 seconds, athletes switch roles.
7	40	10	
9	40	10	
10	30	20	
11	30	20	Continuous exercising.
12	30	20	

14	40	20	
15	40	20	Athletes continually switch roles.
29	40	20	

16	30	10	
17	30	10	Continuous exercising.
19	30	10	

23	60	30	After 30 seconds, athletes switch roles.
41	60	20	

42	120	45	
47	90	45	
48	120	60	
49	40	20	Continuous exercising.
55	60	45	
57	60	20	Right arm.
57	60	20	Left arm.

58	40	20	
59	40	20	
60	40	20	After 20 seconds, athletes switch roles.
63	40	20	
66	40	20	

73	40	25	
75	40	25	
79	30	30	
80	30	30	
81	40	30	
82	40	30	Continuous exercising.
83	30	30	
84	30	30	
88	60	45	
89	60	45	
92	60	45	

95	60	45	
99	60	45	Right leg.
99	60	45	Left leg.
100	120	-	

Table 9   Example of a programme to develop both psycho-motor abilities and fitness. Duration of exercising is approximately 30 min.

Exercise	Duration of Exercise (in sec.)	Rest Between Exercises (in sec.)	Notes	
2	40	15		
3	40	15		
6	40	15	Athletes	
4	40	15	change	With both
			roles	hands.
4	40	15	after 20	With left hand.
4	40	15	seconds.	With right hand.
7	40	15		With right hand.
7	40	15		With left hand.
9	40	15		With right hand.
9	40	15		With left hand.
49	30	20	Continuous exercising.	
54	30	10	Athletes	Both hands.
54	30	10	switch roles	Right hand.
54	30	10	after15	Left hand.
			seconds.	
56	60	20	Athletes	Right fist.
56	60	20	switch	Left fist.
57	60	20	roles	Right arm.
57	60	20	after 30	Left arm.
78	60	20	seconds.	

14	30	15		Hitting with right hand.
14	30	15	Continuous Exercising.	Hitting with left hand.
14	30	15		On right leg, hitting right.
14	30	15	Continuous exercising.	On right leg, hitting left.
14	30	15	Practice.	On left leg, hitting right.
14	30	15		On left leg, hitting left.
16	30	15		Arms held out front.
16	30	15		Arms held to the side.
16	30	15		Arms held at the neck.
19	30	15		
26	30	15		Hold right.
26	30	15		Hold left.
15	40	15		On both legs.
15	40	15		On right leg.
15	40	-		On left leg.

Exercise Pool

Exercises To Develop Reaction

1   Catching feet

The opponents sit facing each other, their legs stretched out and raised off the floor (fig. 1). B starts out with his feet together about 50 cm above A's feet, which are apart. B tries to bring his feet to the ground while A tries to react quickly and bring his legs together to catch his opponent's lower legs or feet (fig. 2). During the exercise, A may only bring his legs together. He may not lower or raise outstretched legs.

2   Catching hands

The opponents stand facing each other with legs slightly apart. A stretches his arms out in front, with his palms about 50 cm apart. B tries to push his own outstretched arms down between A's arms (fig. 1). A tries to prevent this by bringing his hands together quickly (fig. 2). During the exercise, A may not raise or lower his outstretched arms.
The exercise may also be done sitting (figs. 3 and 4).

3 Hitting thighs

The opponents sit facing each other. A places his palms on his opponent's thighs. B, whose hands are beside his thighs, tries to hit the back of A's hands (figs. 1, 2 and 4). A must react quickly to avoid B's slaps by pulling his hands back and so make B hit himself on his own thighs. Should A pull his hands back before B removes his hands from his thighs, A loses a point.

The exercise may also be done squatting.

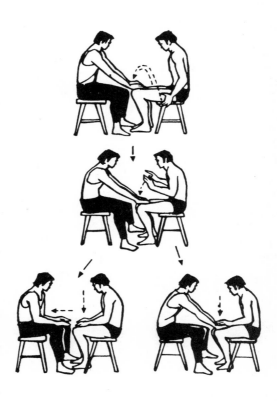

4　Catch the bird

The opponents stand facing each other. A stretches both arms
out in front of him and holds in each fist a small object, such as
a stone, table tennis ball, ball of paper, or coin; B stands ready
with his arms to his sides (fig. 1). A suddenly opens one of his fists
and lets the object fall. B must try to catch it with both hands (fig.
2). The exercise can be made more difficult by having B catch the
object with only his right or left hand.
The exercise may also be done sitting.

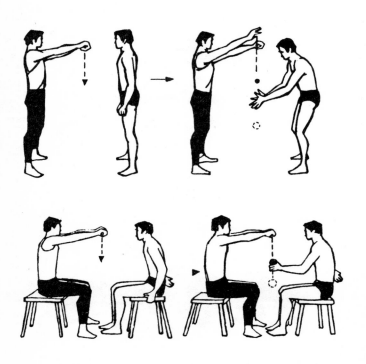

---

5 Push-up match

The opponents face each other in push-up position and try to hit each other's hands (figs. 1 and 2). Both opponents may move in any direction to slap and to avoid slaps, but their trunks and legs must be kept completely stretched.
This exercise is especially engaging when deceptive manoeuvres are used.

6   Slapping hands

The opponents stand facing each other, arms outstretched with palms touching (fig. 1). A, whose palms are underneath, tries to slap the back of B's hands (fig. 2). If he is able to do so (fig. 3), he receives one point. If B is able to avoid the slap by pulling his hands back (fig. 4), he is awarded the point. A may also get a point if B pulls his hands back before A has broken contact with B's palms.
The exercise may also be done sitting.

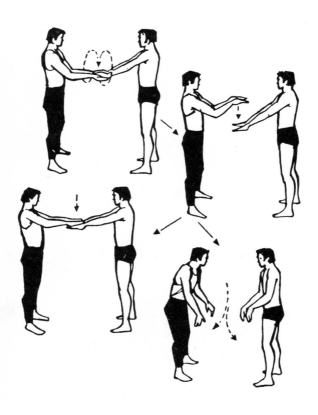

7   Catch the mouse

The opponents stand facing each other with either their right or left arms stretched forward. A's palm faces up, holding a small object, such as a stone, ball of paper, table tennis ball, or coin, (fig. 1); B's palm faces down about 30 cm above A's open hand. B tries to grab the object by lowering his arm quickly and closing his hand on the object (fig. 2). A tries to prevent this by closing his hand (fig. 3). Whoever has the object after each attempt gets a point.
The exercise may also be done sitting.

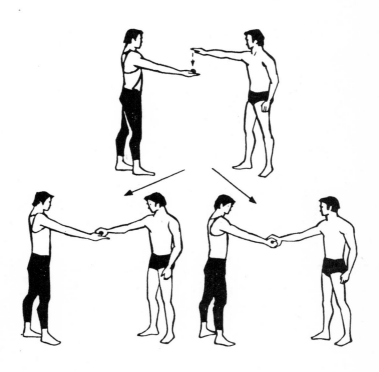

8   Catching the head and neck

A squats in front of B, elbows on thighs and his forearms held so that his palms are about 50 cm apart. B assumes a deep bench position, i.e., his upper arms and forearms and his thighs and lower legs form acute angles (fig. 1). B tries to straighten his arms suddenly and lift up his head so it slips through A's hands (fig. 2). A tries to prevent B from doing so by bringing his hands together (fig. 3). A may not raise his forearms or hands.
The exercise may also be done with A sitting on a stool in front of B (fig. 4).

9 Hold the bird

The opponents stand facing each other with either their right or left arms stretched forward, palms up. A small object, such as a stone, table tennis ball, ball of paper, or coin, is on A's open hand. B, whose hand is about 25 cm lower, tries to hit the object out of A's hand by moving quickly (figs. 1 and 2). A tries to prevent this by closing his hand (fig. 3).
The exercise may also be done sitting.

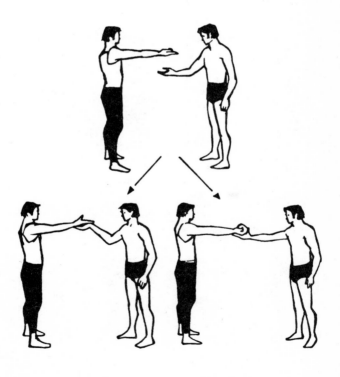

10   Fight to touch feet

The opponents stand facing each other, legs slightly apart, either holding on to each other's elbows with both hands (fig. 1), touching each other only at the shoulders (fig. 3), or not touching at all (fig. 4). Within a set time they try to step as often as possible lightly on each other's feet. Each success earns a point.
This exercise is especially interesting when deceptive manoeuvres are used.

11 Fight to touch shoulders

The opponents stand about 50 cm apart in upright fighting position, with or without hand grip (figs. 1 and 4), and attempt to hit each other lightly on the shoulders as often as possible within a set time. Both opponents may move in any direction. Each successful touch (figs. 2 and 3) is worth one point. Should their heads touch, however, both players lose a point.
The exercise is especially interesting when deceptive manoeuvres are used.

12 Fight to touch thighs

The opponents stand about 50 cm apart in bent fighting position, with or without hand grip (figs. 1 and 3), and attempt to hit each other lightly on the thigh or buttock as often as possible within a set time. Both opponents may move in any direction. Each successful touch (figs. 2 and 4) is worth one point.

The exercise is especially interesting when deceptive manoeuvres are used.

---

13   Step sideways

The opponents stand about 80 cm apart facing the same direction, clasp hands and walk (fig. 1), run or jump (fig. 2) in a circle. When a signal such as a whistle, call, clap of hands, or light is given, each pulls on his opponent's arm quickly in order to force him to take a step sideways (fig. 3).

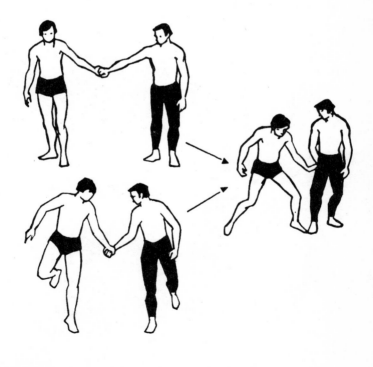

Exercises To Develop Balance

14   Hold tight!

The opponents stand heel to toe on a line facing each other. A raises one arm and holds it out to the side (fig. 1). B bends both arms at the elbow and crosses his forearms at chest level so that his hands are held firmly, palms out, about 10 cm away from his face (fig. 4). A then hits at the right or left palm of his opponent (fig. 2), trying to make him step off the line (fig. 3). By locking his hands, B prevents A from touching his face.
The exercise may also be done standing on one foot.

---

15 . Line fight

The opponents stand heel to toe on a line facing each other, with either their right or left arms raised and held out to the side (fig. 1). They hit their raised hands hard against each other (fig. 2), each trying to force the other's feet off the line (fig. 3).

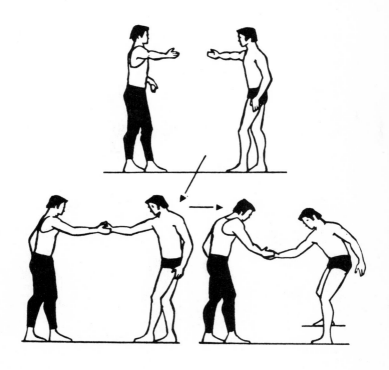

15a Line fight

Exercise 15 may also be done standing on one foot (fig. 1). By hitting the other's hand (fig. 2), each attempts to force his opponent off the line or onto both legs (fig. 3).

16   Straddle fight

The opponents stand facing each other, legs spread far apart. The arms are bent so that the palms touch at eye level (fig. 1), arms are stretched to the side, palms touching (fig. 2), or hands are clasped behind the head, elbows touching (fig. 3). By pressing, each opponent tries to force the other to change his standing position, that is, to cause him to take a step back (fig. 4).

The exercise may also be done standing on one leg, trying to force the opponent to step back or onto both legs.

17   Squatting fight

The opponents squat about 50 cm apart. The arms are bent so that the palms touch at eye level (fig. 1); arms are stretched to the side, palms touching (fig. 2); or hands are clasped behind the head, elbows touching (fig. 3). By pressing, each attempts to force his opponent to jump backwards or to roll onto his back (fig. 4).
A soft surface is necessary for this exercise.

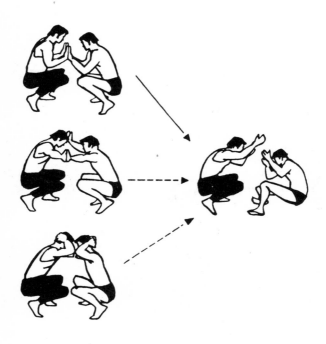

18   Frog fight and crab fight

Opponents begin in a deep kneebend position, their arms in front, slightly bent at the elbows (fig. 1). Within a set time, both opponents try to knock each other off balance by pushing against the other's arms or body. During this exercise each athlete may jump in the deep kneebend to the side or behind his opponent (figs. 2 and 3). In the crab fight both opponents face each other in backwards push-up position, with either left or right legs raised, feet touching. Each opponent then tries to knock the other off balance (figs. 4 and 5).
A soft surface is necessary for this exercise.

19   Hitting buttocks, shoulder or chest

The opponents stand together in straddle position either with buttocks touching (fig. 1) or chest to chest (fig. 3), or they stand side to side with legs almost closed and shoulders touching (fig. 5). By pushing hard where their bodies meet, each opponent tries to force the other to take a step forwards (fig. 2), or backwards (fig. 4), or to lift his foot (fig. 5).

20   Cross-legged fight

The opponents sit cross-legged 20 to 30 cm apart (fig. 1) and each attempts to force his opponent onto his back (fig. 2) by pressing against his arms and body. Touching the opponent's head and hitting are not allowed.
A soft surface is necessary for this exercise.

21   Sole fight

The opponents sit balanced on their buttocks with legs up, knees bent and the soles of their feet pressed together; arms are folded on their chests (fig. 1). By straightening the legs powerfully, each opponent tries to make the other roll onto his back (fig. 2).

22   Side push-up fight

The opponents face each other in side push-up position about 50 cm apart and each attempts to push the other off balance with his hands (fig. 2). Legs stay together throughout the exercise.

23   Riding the camel

B begins in the bench position. A sits on B's back with his lower legs and feet folded behind B's thighs (fig. 1). B then attempts to throw A off by straightening his legs repeatedly. A tries to prevent himself from being thrown by raising his arms to the side and stretching his chest and hips forward (fig. 2).

24 Headstand fight

Opponents are back to back in headstand position, 10 to 20 cm apart (fig. 1). Each tries to upset the other's balance and bring him into bench position (fig. 4) by pushing with his feet (fig. 2), lower legs or buttocks.

This exercise is often called the "candle" and may also be done from the shoulderstand position (figs. 5 and 6).

25 Lizard fight

The opponents face each other in front push-up position (fig. 1). Each tries to bring the other onto his stomach (fig. 3) by grasping the wrist (fig. 2) and pulling powerfully. While their legs, trunk and arms must remain as fully stretched as possible, both opponents may move in all directions on their hands and feet in order to attack or to escape.

26   Foot lift

The opponents stand sideways to each other, grasping hands as if to shake and placing the outside of their forward feet together (fig. 1). Each pushes or pulls hard to make the other lift his front or back leg (fig. 2).
The exercise may be varied by having the athletes face each other, grasping both hands (figs. 3 and 4).

27   Balancing dance and Boundary fight

The opponents stand on one leg facing each other and grasping hands. Each pulls and pushes with his arms while jumping in all directions to force his opponent onto both legs.

This exercise can be made more difficult by instructing each opponent to force the other to jump or step over a "boundary" line (figs. 3 and 4). The opponents may hop around only within their own areas.

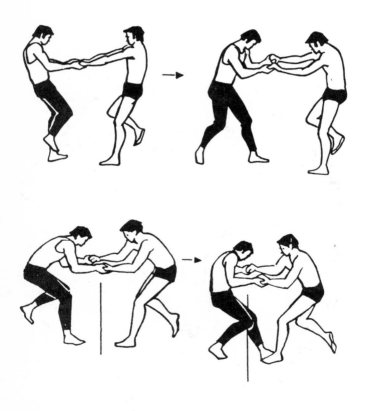

28   Locked arms fight

Standing side by side, the opponents link arms, clasping their own hands tightly (fig. 1). Each opponent tries to force the other to change his position, i.e., to lift a leg or to take a step, by bending the trunk, by moving the arms or by turning the body (fig. 2). The exercise may be carried out by using leg hooks also. The object of this variation is to make the opponent touch the floor with a part of his body other than his feet (figs. 3 and 4).

29   Foot sweep

Standing side by side and facing in the same direction, the opponents place their arms around each other's shoulder and neck. A puts his lower calf against B's lower shin, both straighten their legs and raise their feet from the floor (fig. 1). B then tries to make A roll onto his back by lifting forwards (fig. 2), while A tries to make B touch the floor with his hand by lifting backwards (fig. 3).

30   Lock fight and foot-lifting fight

The opponents each stand on one leg and face in opposite directions, their raised legs and arms locked together (fig. 1). Each tries to put the other onto his back by pulling and pushing hard with the arms, legs and shoulders (fig. 2).
In the foot-lifting fight, the opponents begin by holding each other behind the neck with one hand and by the ankle with the other hand. The object is to make one's opponent fall by lifting his leg and by pulling on his arm or neck (figs. 3 and 4).
(pp. 60-78: Exercises to develop orientation and adaption)

Exercises To Develop Orientation and Adaptation

31   Rolling opponent from stomach to back

B lies on his stomach. A sits at his side and must roll B onto his back within a certain time. In order to do this, A can reach under his opponent's arm to grasp his neck or head (fig. 1). By lifting up his opponent's upper arm while pressing his head or neck down, A may roll B onto his back (fig. 2).

A can also reach under B's arm to grasp his neck, while sliding his other hand under B's near thigh to grasp his far thigh (fig. 3). By pulling hard with both hands (fig. 4), A can roll B onto his shoulders.

32 Rolling opponent from beneath

B lies on his back. A sits beside him and grasps B's upper arm with one hand while reaching across B's body to grab his shoulder from under the armpit (fig. 1) or to encircle his neck (fig. 2). B must reverse this position in a set time, by putting both arms around his opponent's trunk, bringing his opponent's centre of gravity as close as possible to his own, and turning his body along its axis (fig. 3), bringing his opponent with him. In this way, B will assume the upper position (fig. 4)

A soft surface is required for this exercise.

33   Moving from stomach to bench position

B lies on his stomach and is controlled by A, who is beside and behind him (fig. 1). B's objective is to reach bench position within a set time and against his opponent's resistance. He may do this by pushing his knees forward (fig. 2) and by straightening his arms (fig. 3). The exercise may also be done while A lies on B's back without holding on to him, but offering resistance. B tries to reach bench position or to throw A off, but B must not move his hands and feet from the floor.

34 Breaking opponent to stomach from bench position

B starts in bench position. A's task is to take B to his stomach within a set time. To do this, A should grasp B's trunk and nearest arm (fig. 1) and pull him down toward where his arm support had been (fig. 2). Another way is to grasp B around the trunk with one arm while grasping his near wrist with the other hand. By pushing his head against B's armpit and by pulling on his wrist, A can take him down to his stomach (figs. 3 and 4). A third possibility is to lift the opponent's arm at the elbow, grasp his back and push toward where the arm had been (figs. 5 and 6).

35   Grasping trunk

A starts in bench position. B kneels beside and behind him and, within a set time, must put both arms around A's trunk with or without locking an arm. A prevents this by blocking B's wrist (fig. 1) and by dropping to his stomach (fig. 2). B can overcome A's defensive position by releasing his wrists and by pulling hard on A's upper arms (figs. 3 and 4), thus putting himself back in position to clasp both arms around A's trunk (fig. 5).

Another technique to use when one's opponent is on his stomach is to pull up on his chin (figs. 6-8).

36 Rolling opponent from bench position to back

B starts in bench position. A kneels down beside him and must roll B onto his back within a set time. In order to do so, A grasps both of B's arms (fig. 1), pulls them hard towards himself (fig. 2), and by pressing with his shoulders, forces B onto his back (fig. 3). A variation is to grasp both of B's legs (fig. 4), pull them in hard (fig. 5) and then roll the opponent onto his back (fig. 6).
A soft surface is necessary for this exercise.

37   Turning on the floor

A starts in bench position or on his stomach. B controls him from the side and back (fig. 1 or 6). Against resistance and within a set time, A must reach the upper position and, in turn, control his opponent from the side and back. In order to do this, A can lift up and grasp his opponent's wrist at his stomach and his opponent's upper arm (fig. 1), getting up on his knees and twisting (figs. 2 to 5). When on his stomach, A can push up on his hands and knees (figs. 6 and 7), turn his opponent slightly (fig. 8) and twist away to control his opponent from behind (fig. 9).

38   Floor wrestling

B starts in bench position. A kneels beside and behind him, with both hands placed on B's back (fig. 1). The match begins following a signal (whistle, call, clap of hands) (fig. 2). Within a set time, A must force B onto his shoulders (see also Exercise 36). He should try to bring B onto his stomach (see Exercise 34) and then roll him onto his back (see Exercise 31). The match is over when B has been forced onto both shoulders, or when B has reached upper position by turning on his opponent (see also Exercise 37) to control him from the side and behind.

Both players must keep at least one knee or lower leg on the floor during the exercise.

Floor wrestling is an exercise which not only teaches orientation techniques and adaption but is also highly effective in developing coordination and conditioning. Because the opponent is never thrown, there is reduced danger of injury.

A soft surface is necessary for this exercise.

39   Wrestling on knees

The opponents begin by facing each other on their knees with their hands on each other's shoulders (fig. 1). Each athlete must try to force the other onto both shoulders without rising to his feet. This may be accomplished by rolling in front of the opponent and by pulling on his head and upper arm (figs. 2 and 3).
A variation of this exercise is to try to pull the opponent forward and down and make him touch the floor with a part of his body other than his legs (figs. 4 and 5).

40 Standing from bench position

B begins in the bench position and is controlled by A, who is beside and behind him (fig. 1). B must try to rise to his feet within a set time and against A's resistance. This can be done by putting one foot down on the floor under the opponent's body (fig. 2) and straightening up forcefully (fig. 3), or by first grasping and then pushing away his opponent's wrists (figs. 4 to 7).

41   Hunt in the darkness

Both opponents stand in a fighting area. B's eyes are blindfolded
(fig. 1). A calls to B at specific intervals. B tries to grab hold of A
(who may not leave the fighting area), hold on to him and touch
a specific part of his body, such as the knee, foot or thigh (fig. 2).
After two to three minutes the athletes switch roles, i.e., A
becomes the catcher and B the runner.
The player who has touched his opponent most often within the
alloted time is the winner.
Because the eyes cannot be used to orient the athlete, this
exercise improves one's sense of touch and motion.

42   Fight in the darkness

Both opponents are blindfolded. Standing in a fighting area 3 to 6 m in diameter, they must turn around three times (fig. 1) and then try to grasp each other (fig. 2) and force or carry the other out of the circle (fig.3). The opponent who leaves the circle first is the loser.
This exercise may be varied so that the objective is to grasp the opponent and touch a specific part of his body (fig. 4; see Exercise 41).

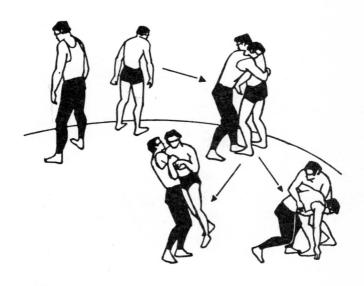

43 Reaching opponent's starting position

The opponents stand 5 to 10 m apart on a marked path (fig. 1) and each attempts to reach the other's starting position first. This exercise may be varied by having each opponent attempt to carry the other back to his starting position (figs. 2 and 3).

44   Race through the ravine

The opponents stand about 5 m apart on a marked path (fig. 1). B, the runner, must reach the end of the pathway as quickly as possible. A, the catcher, stands in the middle of the path and tries to block B as long as possible with his arms spread out (figs. 2 and 3). A may not hold B. B is awarded one point if he reaches the end of the pathway within the allotted time. After the exercise has been completed, the opponents switch roles, i.e., A becomes the runner and B, the catcher.

45   Moving behind opponent's back

The opponents stand face to face. Within a set time, each tries to move behind the other's back. This can be done by holding and pulling hard on the opponent's upper arm (figs. 1 and 2), by blocking and dropping underneath the opponent's upper arm (figs. 3 and 4) or by dropping down and pulling on the opponent's thigh (figs. 5 to 8).

46   Grasping and lifting opponent's leg

The opponents may stand either far apart (fig. 1) or close together (fig. 5). Each tries to grasp the other's leg and lift it from the floor. This can be done by grasping and pulling the opponent's forearm upwards and then dropping down and away from him (figs. 2 to 4), by pulling the opponent's upper arm upwards and by dropping quickly in front of him (figs. 6 to 9) or by dropping underneath the opponent's armpits (figs. 10 to 14).

47 Wrestling for the treasure

The opponents begin standing or on their knees facing each other, with either one or both hands around an object (ball, sport pole, etc.) Each tries to wrest the "treasure" from his opponent. For this exercise, care must be taken that objects are used that will not cause any injury to the contestants.

48   Upper body or belt wrestling

The opponents stand facing each other, either holding on to each other (fig. 3) or with their hands on each other's belts (fig. 1). Each tries to lift the other from the floor (figs. 2 and 4) to make him touch the floor with a part of his body other than his feet (fig. 5), to force him out of the fighting area or to move behind his back (fig. 6). In belt wrestling only one hand may be removed from the belt. Only those trained to do so should be allowed to throw an opponent from standing position to the ground, because of the risk of injury.

49 Fight to remain standing or sitting

A stands at a right angle to B, who is seated with knees bent. A grasps his opponent's hand and places the outside of his front foot against the tips of his opponent's toes (fig. 1). A must pull B so that his buttocks rise off the floor (fig. 3), while B tries to pull A forward and down until his back leg raises off the floor (fig. 2). After each contest the opponents change places.

50   Pulling opponent from sitting position and Finger stretching

The opponents either sit face to face, holding on to each other's hands, with legs straight and the soles of the feet placed against each other (fig. 1), or they sit on benches, sides of the feet together (fig. 3). Each opponent tries to raise the other off the ground or off the bench by pulling hard with his arms and by using his buttocks to bend his trunk backwards (figs. 2 and 4).

Pulling matches from a sitting position may also be used to develop finger strength. The opponents lock one finger together and each tries to lift his opponent from his seat or make his opponent straighten out his finger. All fingers on the right and left hands should be used one after the other.

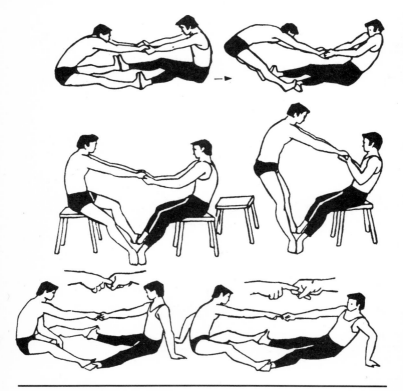

51　Stepping forwards and Lifting the treasure

Opponents stand face to face in a right or left walking position, holding each other's forward hand and with the tips of their forward toes placed against each other (fig. 1). Each opponent must try to force the other to take a step forward by pulling hard, being careful not to lose his own footing (fig. 2).

In "lifting the treasure" (fig. 3), similar objects, such as stones, cloths, or poles are placed behind each opponent on the floor. The opponent who picks up his "treasure first" or causes his opponent to take a step is the winner.

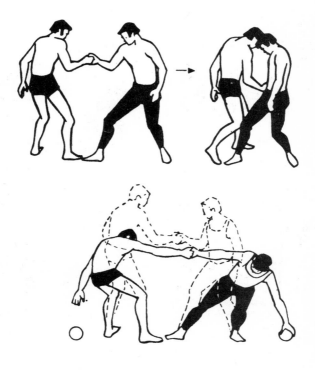

52   Pulling opponent into the circle or over the line

The opponents stand opposite each other outside a circle approximately 50 cm in diameter, holding one or both of each other's hands above the circle (fig. 1). Each then tries to pull the other into the circle (fig. 2).
When the exercise is to pull the opponent over a line, the players may move as they please on their side of the line.
Belt pulling is a variation of this exercise. Instead of gripping hands, a belt is placed over opponents' necks. Whoever is pulled over the line or who has the belt slip off his head is the loser.

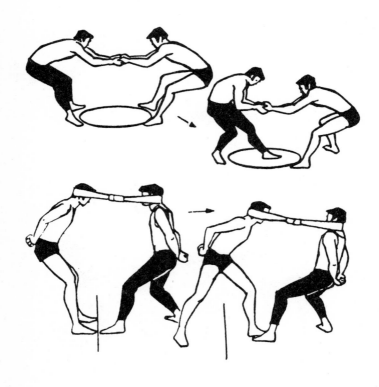

53   Fight to remain standing (II)

The opponents stand facing each other, arms bent and clasping
each other's raised hands (fig. 1). By bending the other's hands
back against his forearms and by straightening one's arms at the
elbow, each opponent tries to force the other to kneel.
The player wins who forces his opponent down so far that his
thighs and lower legs form an acute angle (fig. 2).
The exercise may be varied with one partner attempting to raise
himself within a set time from a deep kneebend (fig. 2) to standing
(fig. 1). For this variation, after each contest the opponents
switch roles.

54   Escape

The opponents either stand or sit facing each other. B grasps his opponent's forearm with both hands (fig. 1) or grasps both of his opponent's wrists (fig. 2). A tries to break the hold quickly (within 2 to 4 seconds) by turning his hands and putting pressure on the opponent's thumb (fig. 3).

The opponents may also practice freeing themselves from any other type of grip (figs. 4 and 5).

After the exercise has been carried out one or more times, the opponents switch roles.

55   Neck pulling in push-up position

The opponents begin facing each other in push-up position; each has one hand around the other's neck (fig. 1). By pulling or pushing forward and down or sideways each tries to force the other onto his stomach (fig. 2). In performing this exercise the athletes may move in all directions. If a player releases his hand from the other's neck, he loses.

This exercise can be varied so that the opponents must pull each other a specified distance. In this variation, they must fight with their heads raised, to prevent the opponent's hand from slipping. A third variation combines the options described above. The player who puts his opponent on his stomach or who pulls him a specified distance is the winner.

56   Fist out of the circle

The opponents lie facing each other on their stomachs with their corresponding forearm and fist placed inside a circle about 50 cm in diameter (fig. 1). Each tries to force his opponent's fist out of the circle. Forearms and fists may not move off the floor (fig. 2). This exercise may also be done sitting, with the opponent's forearms and fists lying on a hard surface, such as a table top or trunk. The object is to push the fist of one's opponent from the surface (figs. 3 and 4).

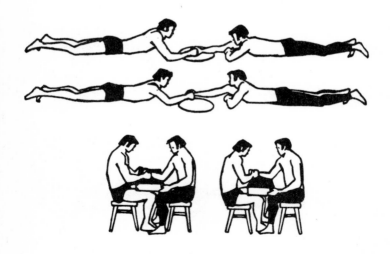

57   Arm wrestling

The opponents lie on their stomachs facing each other, with arms bent at right angles, elbows on the floor and hands clasped (fig. 1). Each tries to force the other's hand to the floor (fig. 2). Elbows may not be lifted from the floor.
This exercise may also be done sitting or kneeling with elbows placed on a hard surface or on one's thighs.

58   Hands up and hands together

The opponents stand facing each other. B has his hands around opponent's arms and trunk (fig. 1). A then tries, within a specified time (2 to 8 seconds), to bring his hands together over his head against B's resistance (figs. 2 and 3).

After each contest, the opponents switch roles.

In the "hands together" variation, B grasps both of his opponent's wrists. A then tries to bring his hands together against B's resistance.

After the exercise has been carried out one or more times, the opponents switch roles.

59   Hands to the sides

A raises his arms above his head and B puts his arms around A's upper arms and neck (fig. 1). Within a specified time (4 to 8 seconds), A must bring his hands down to his thighs against B's resistance (figs. 2 and 3).

60   Knee on the floor

B holds his opponent's arms high up in the air (fig. 1). Within a specified time (4 to 8 seconds), A must touch the floor with one knee (fig. 2).

61   Lifting opponent by the arm

A stands with his back to B, who has one arm over A's shoulders; A grasps B's arm above the elbow with both hands (fig. 1). Within a specified time (3 to 5 seconds), A must lift B off the ground by pulling hard on B's upper arm and by bending forward while straightening his legs (fig. 3). B tries to keep from being lifted off the ground by lowering his centre of gravity (fig. 2).

A variation of this exercise is to grasp both of the opponent's arms (figs. 4 to 6).

After each contest the opponents switch roles.

62   Lifting opponent from behind

This exercise may be done from standing or prone positions. B stands or squats behind A, with both his arms around A's trunk (figs. 1 and 4). B must lift A off the floor within a specified time (4 to 8 seconds) by straightening his legs and by bending his trunk up and back (figs. 3 and 7). A tries to keep from being lifted off the ground by lowering his centre of gravity.

63   Lifting opponent from the front

The opponents stand facing each other, A's arms around B's trunk (fig. 1): A tries to lift his opponent off the ground within a specified time (4 to 8 seconds) by straightening his legs and by bending his trunk back (fig. 3). B defends by lowering his centre of gravity to keep his feet on the floor (fig. 2).
This exercise is more difficult if A has to lift B off the ground from a kneeling position (figs. 4 to 6).
After the exercise has been carried out one or more times, the opponents switch roles.

64   Lifting opponent by the trunk

The opponents stand, each with his arms clasped around the other's trunk from above (fig. 1) or from the side (fig. 3). Each opponent must try to lift the other off the ground by straightening his legs and trunk (figs. 2 and 4).

65 Lifting opponent from bench position

B starts in the bench position. A squats next to B, facing B's feet and with both arms around B's waist (fig. 1). Within a specified time (4 to 8 seconds, A must lift both B's feet off the floor by straightening up (fig. 3). B tries to prevent being lifted off the floor by shifting his centre of gravity away from his opponent (fig. 2). The exercise may also be done with A having his arms around B's far thigh (figs. 4 and 5).

After each contest the opponents switch roles.

66 Lifting opponent by the thighs

The opponents stand facing each other. A puts both arms around one of B's thighs and tries to lift B off the floor within a specified time (5 to 10 seconds) by straightening up (figs. 1 and 3). B tries to break the hold and keep from being lifted off the ground by moving his legs back (fig. 2).
The exercise may be varied by A grasping both of B's legs. After the exercise has been completed one or more times, the opponents change roles.

67 Leaning sideways fight

The opponents sit back to back with legs stretched out and arms locked together (fig. 1). Each opponent tries to lean over and touch the floor on a specified side with his shoulder (fig. 2). The exercise may also be done with both opponents kneeling face to face, arms around each other and locking one arm (fig. 3). Each player tries to press his opponent to the floor in the direction of his locked arm (fig. 4).

68   Back fight

The opponents stand back to back, clasping each other's hands high above their heads (fig. 1). Each tries to lift his opponent off the ground by lowering his arms and bending his trunk forward (fig. 2).
The exercise may also be done with elbows locked together (figs. 3 and 4).

69   Breaking opponent from backward riding position

B starts in the bench position with A sitting astraddle him facing B's feet and the insteps of both feet tucked under B's thigh (fig. 1). Within a specified time (5 to 10 seconds), A must force B onto his stomach (fig. 3) by lifting his lower legs and feet upwards and by bending his trunk backward (fig. 2). B attempts to maintain the bench position by pressing with his arms in a powerful counter-movement.

After each contest, the athletes switch roles.

A soft surface is necessary for this exercise.

70   Breaking opponent from forward riding position

B starts in the bench position. A. sits on his opponent's lower back with legs tucked under his opponent's thighs (fig. 1). Within a specified time (5 to 10 seconds), A attempts to force B onto his stomach by swinging his trunk forward and by lifting his lower legs (fig. 2). If B manages to maintain his bench position by bracing his arms, A can grasp one of his wrists with both hands (fig. 3) and pull forward (fig. 4).

After each contest, the opponents change roles.

A soft surface is required for this exercise.

71 Sideways roll

B starts in the bench position. A kneels beside and behind him, with both arms around his waist (fig. 1). Within a specific time (8 to 12 seconds), A must roll B onto his right or left side (figs. 2 to 5). B tries to prevent this by shifting his centre of gravity away from his opponent and by bracing his arms (fig. 2). The use of feigning movements to opposite sides helps develop better reaction, orientation and correction abilities.
After each contest, the athletes switch roles.

72   Heels off the floor

Opponents sit at right angles to each other with legs out-
stretched. A's lower legs lie across his opponent's lower legs.
Within a specified time, B must lift his legs from the floor against
A's resistance.

73   Fight to remain swaying

The opponents sit in swaying position facing each other with legs
together. Using the sides of their feet, both try to force the other's
legs to the ground.
The athletes may not open or bend their legs.

.74   Legs to the floor

The opponents sit facing each other, leaning back on their arms, corresponding legs raised and placed together below the ankles (fig. 1). Each opponent then tries to force the other's raised leg sideways onto the floor (fig. 2).
A variation of this exercise, often referred to as the "candle", may be carried out back to back from a shoulderstand (figs. 3 and 4).

75 Leg lock

The opponents lie on their backs facing opposite directions with shoulders touching and adjoining arms locked together (fig. 1). The opponents swing up and lower their legs twice (fig. 2). The third time, they lock knees and each tries to force the other to roll backward by pressing down (figs. 3 and 4).
After each contest, the athletes should change sides, ensuring that both legs are exercised equally.

76   Closing opponent's legs (standing)

The opponents stand shoulder to shoulder, adjoining hands placed on each other's necks and adjoining legs raised with the sides of the feet together (fig. 1). Each player tries to close his opponent's legs together by pushing out powerfully (fig. 2).
The exercise may also be done chest to chest (fig. 3), so that one player tries to close the other's legs together (fig. 4). After this variation has been attempted one or more times, the opponents switch roles.

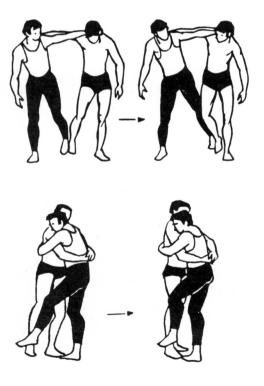

77   Closing opponent's legs (lying)

The opponents sit in swaying position facing each other, leaning back on their hands for support, and legs open wide (figs. 1). A, whose insteps are placed against the outsides of his opponent's lower legs, tries within a specified time to bring his opponent's legs together by closing his own legs (fig. 2).

A variation of this exercise can be done lying face down (figs. 3 and 4). It can also be carried out using resistance; i.e., B begins with his legs together and must bring his feet apart against resistance applied by A. The opponents switch roles after the exercise has been carried out one or more times.

78   Knee and hand presses

The opponents sit facing each other with knees separated (fig. 1). A places the inside of his knees against the outside of B's knees and tries, within a specified time, to bring his opponent's knees together (fig. 2). The exercise may also be carried out so that B tries to bring his knees apart against resistance applied by A.

In "hand pressing", the opponents sit facing each other, arms stretched forward, A's palms against the back of B's hands. A tries to bring his opponent's outstretched palms together (figs. 3 and 4).

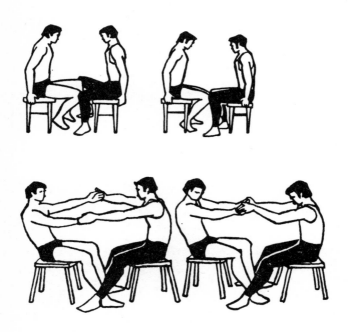

79 Turning around opponent (sitting or from bench position

Opponents sit back to back, legs outstretched or bent (fig. 1), in bench position (fig. 2), or in forward push-up position, head to head. Following a signal, the opponents try to move around each other (fig. 3) and control the other from the side and behind (fig. 4).

80   Turning around opponent (standing)

Opponents stand back to back at attention (fig. 1). Following a signal (whistle, call, clapping hands, flashing light, etc.) each turns around to the left or right and tries to put his arms around his opponent and lift him from the ground.

The exercise may also be done standing chest to chest (fig. 3). Following the signal, each tries to move behind his opponent (fig. 4) and lift him from behind off the floor (fig. 5).

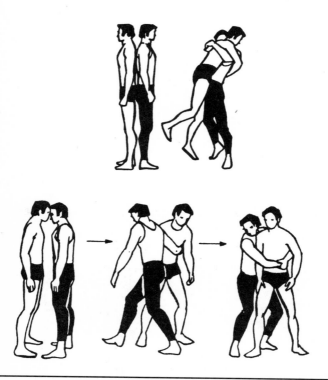

81   Catching opponent

Opponents begin back to back, standing at attention (fig. 1), sitting with their knees up or legs straight, or squatting (fig. 2). One of these athletes is called and must run to a target as quickly as possible while his opponent must turn to follow (fig. 3), catch and hold him, and lift him off the floor (fig. 4) before the target is reached.

Finish

82   Fight to sit up

The opponents lie on their backs, feet pointing in opposite directions and knees touching; their arms are folded over their chest (fig. 1). Following a signal, each athlete stretches his arms out and forward, straightens up at the waist and tries to prevent his opponent from sitting up also (fig. 2). It is important to bring the arms forward in order to avoid hitting heads.

The exercise may also be done lying back to back (fig. 3). After the signal, the athletes must sit up without using their hands, keeping their legs straight, and try to prevent the opponent from straightening up by using only the hand nearest the opponent. Use of the other hand for support disqualifies the athlete.

83   Side push-up pursuit

The opponents start in side push-up position facing each other, right or left hands resting in a circle about 50 cm in diameter marked on the floor (fig. 1). Following a signal, each opponent runs as quickly as possible in a circle around his support hand until he can hit his opponent on the waist or buttock (fig. 2).
A player loses when he is hit, if his support hand leaves the circle, or if he touches the floor with a part of his body other than his support hand and feet.

84   Clock tag

The opponents start in front push-up position (fig. 1), the soles of their feet placed against each other at the centre of a circle about 50 cm in diameter. Following a signal, each opponent runs in a circle as quickly as possible in one direction until he can hit his opponent on the back or chest (fig. 2).

A player loses when he is hit, if his feet leave the circle, or if a part of his body other than his hands and feet touch the floor.

A variation of this exercise is useful to develop reaction, orientation and correction abilities. One athlete is made the catcher, his opponent the runner. In order to hit or to avoid being hit, catcher and runner may change direction as often as they want.

85   Tag

The opponents start face to face or back to back in a 20 to 60 square meter fighting area, either standing (fig. 1), kneeling, squatting, or in push-up position (fig. 3). One athlete is designated as the catcher, his opponent as the runner. Within a set time (8 to 15 seconds) and using a specified type of movement, e.g., running or jumping, the catcher tries to reach the runner and hit a specified part of his body (figs. 2 and 4). The catcher receives a point for each hit, but loses a point should his type of movement change.
After the allotted time, the athletes switch roles.

86   Getting past the barrier

The opponents stand facing each other about 5 m apart on a path which has been marked on the floor (fig. 1). B must reach the end of the path without being hit by A on a specified point on his body (fig. 2). Neither athlete may leave the marked path during the exercise.

After each contest, the opponents switch roles.

Exercises To Develop Endurance

87   Pursuit

The opponents start on opposite sides outside a marked area 15 to 25 m in diameter. Following a signal each opponent runs around the area in one direction for a set time and tries to catch up with the other and hit a specified point on his body. Players may not step into the marked surface. If neither opponent has hit the other, the runner who has come closest to his opponent's back is the winner.

The exercise can be made more difficult by changing the way the players move, e.g., jumping on one or both legs; running backward, in push-up position, squatting, etc.

This exercise can be further varied to develop coordination. One opponent is designated as the catcher, another as the runner. In order to hit or to avoid being hit, both may change direction whenever they wish.

88   Tug-of-war

The opponents stand facing each other, holding one (fig. 1) or both hands (fig. 2). Within a set time (up to 3 minutes), each attempts to move out of the fighting area or to pull his opponent a set distance (5 to 15 meters). The player wins who crosses the boundary line or who pulls his opponent across the specified distance most often before the time is up. If neither objective is met, whoever has pulled his opponent across a greater distance is the winner.

Tug-of-war with one hand can be combined with "lifting the treasure" (exercise 51). Now, however, the objects are placed much further away from the opponents. The further away the objects are, the more difficult the contest becomes. The first one to pick up the object is the winner.

89　Neck pulling

The opponents stand facing each other, with hands around each other's necks. Within a set time (up to 3 minutes), each tries to move out of the fighting area in spite of his opponent's resistance (figure 1 below), or tries to pull his opponent across a set distance. The opponents may not release their hands from each other's necks.
The winner is determined as in exercise 88.

90　Backwards tug-of-war

The opponents stand back to back, hands joined. Against his opponent's resistance, each tries to move from the fighting area (fig. 2) or to pull the other across a set distance (5 to 15 m). The player who crosses the boundary line most often in the time allotted or who pulls his opponent the whole distance or the greatest distance is the winner.

91   Tug-of-war through legs

The opponents stand back to back at the centre of a fighting area.
Bending forward, they put their arms between their legs and
clasp hands behind (fig. 1 below). Each opponent tries to get one
foot over the boundary line within a set time (up to 3 minutes).
The winner is determined as in exercise 90.

92   Pushing opponent out of fighting area

Players stand at the centre of a fighting area. One hand grasps
the opponent's upper arm while the other hand is slipped around
the opponent's trunk onto his back. Each tries to push the other
over the boundary line within a set time (up to 3 minutes) (fig. 2).
The first to cross the boundary line or the one who has been
pushed furthest is the loser.

93　Fight to enter the fighting area

A stands inside a fighting area and tries to prevent B, who begins outside this area, from moving inside within a set time (fig. 1 below). A must keep at least one foot inside the area. B must enter the fighting area with both feet to win.

94　Pushing with shoulders

The opponents stand shoulder to shoulder at the centre of a fighting area, with adjacent arms locked together (fig. 2). The player who pushes his opponent over the boundary line within a set time (up to 3 minutes) is the winner.

95   Pushing with backs

Opponents stand back to back at the centre of a fighting area, with both arms locked together (fig. 1 below). The player who can push his opponent so that at least one foot leaves the fighting area within a set time (up to 3 minutes) is the winner. Turning as well as pushing is allowed.

96   Pushing in push-up position

The opponents begin at the centre of a fighting area shoulder to shoulder in forward push-up position (fig. 2). Within a set time, each tries to push the other player out of the fighting area or to force him out of push-up position. A player loses if any part of his body is pushed out of the fighting area or if a part of his body other than his hands or feet touches the floor.

97   Pushing backward in push-up position

The opponents begin at the centre of a fighting area in push-up position. Facing in opposite directions, each player places one leg between his opponent's legs so that they are buttock to buttock (fig. 1). Within a set time, each opponent tries to make the other place a hand across a boundary line or touch the floor with a part of his body other than his hands or feet. The players may push backwards and turn to either side, but may not run forward.

98 Pulling and pushing with legs locked

The opponents stand facing each other on one leg at the centre of a fighting area. They hold on to each other above the elbows and lock their raised legs (fig. 1). Each opponent tries to force the other out of the fighting area as often as possible within a set time (up to 3 minutes) (fig. 2) or to make him touch the floor with a part of his body other than his supporting foot (fig. 3). Each success is worth one point. The player who wins a set number of points or who has the most points when time expires is the winner.

99   Cockfight

The opponents stand facing each other on one leg at the centre
of a fighting area, arms folded across their chests. Each player
tries to force the other onto both legs (fig. 2) or to push him over
the boundary line (fig. 3) by bumping into him or jumping at him
(fig. 1). Opponents should be allowed to switch support legs only
after a set time. Each success is worth one point. The player who
wins a set number of points or who has the most points when time
expires is winner.
The use of deceptive moves helps develop reaction, orientation
and correction abilities.

100 Throwing opponent out of the square

The opponents stand in a square area (4 to 16 m²) and attempt within a set time (up to 3 minutes) to push each other across the boundary lines, which are identified with the numbers 1, 2, 3 and 4. Pushing the opponent over boundary line 1 is worth 1 point; pushing him over boundary line 2 is worth 2 points, etc. The player who wins a set number of points or who has the most points when time expires is the winner.

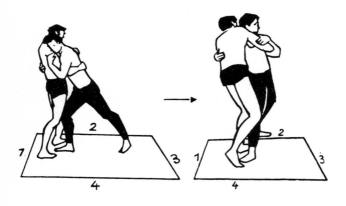

Notes